THE
SUPPORT
VERSES

Earliest Sayings of the Buddha

☙❧

Translated and Adapted by

CHRISTOPHER
CARTER
SANDERSON

Sagging
Meniscus

Parts of *The Support Verses* first appeared, in slightly different form, in *Lunch Ticket Magazine* and *SHIFT*.

Set in Janson with LaTeX.

ISBN: 978-1-952386-26-8 (paperback)
ISBN: 978-1-952386-27-5 (ebook)
Library of Congress Control Number: 2021944561

Sagging Meniscus Press
Montclair, New Jersey
saggingmeniscus.com

One field of flowers makes many bouquets;
One life can do good in many fine ways.

Many thanks
to The Awoke.

Many thanks
to my teachers, past and present.

Many thanks
to my friends at L'Arche Syracuse.

Many thanks
to my editor at Lunch Ticket Magazine, Sona Gevorkian.

For Meredith and Max, my joys.

Translator's Note

"The Support Verses" is my best English translation of the title of *The Dhammapada*, as it is usually transliterated from its original language—Pali, a language older than Sanskrit. While some of the verses in it are in Pali, others have come down to us only in Sanskrit. *The Dhammapada* is the earliest and most ubiquitous collection of The Buddha's sayings in existence across all Buddhist traditions, and has accordingly been translated into English many times over hundreds of years. My purpose in adding another translation is to artistically transmit the truth of the verses as I have received them after meditation and contemplation of them. Therefore, they are in the vocabulary and syntax of my own idiomatic English: sometimes academic and sometimes profane, as needed.

My intention is also to honor the Buddha's—who, by the way, I call "The Awoke" in the translation—suggestion in verse 102 that "one memorable maxim that grants peace outshines all dusty, forgotten volumes." To do this, I use the verse form of the most quoted plays in the English language: iambic pentameter. The Buddha's idea in verse 102 is mirrored by the philosopher Seneca who said: "I'd rather write one memorable maxim than whole volumes of forgotten philosophy." Verse 102 made it clear to me—as did Shakespeare's knowledge of Seneca which informed his writing—that *The Support Verses* were very much meant to be remembered and quoted. Long ago literacy was not widespread and therefore, the catchiness of verses was a present concern for writers. And so, I hope that verses like, "one field of flowers makes many bouquets; one life can do good in many fine ways" will stay in your memory. I sincerely believe it was The Buddha's intention that his sayings should.

In this translation I have taken an unusual step which has granted the verses clarity for me: translating every word of the verses into English, leaving no words of transliterated Pali or Sanskrit. This sidesteps for me any temptation to fetishize foreign terminology. It can be seductive to imagine that enlightenment is a faraway, foreign thing summoned by the pronouncement of exotic-sounding syllables, but it can be spoken in our own tongue and read in our own language; indeed, the Buddha at every instance suggests that enlightenment is nearby, usual, ordinary, and possible for anyone to attain and feel utterly familiar with.

As with any great religious text or poetic work, and *The Support Verses* is both, reading in the original languages and in as many translations as possible will yield deep insight and is to be recommended. My translation/adaptation is by no means definitive or exclusive; it is meant to join the galaxy of translations of this great work, offering readers additional artistic insight and spiritual utility.

Contents

THE
SUPPORT
VERSES

Stanza One

Repetitions

1 The mind gives life shape; we'll be what we think.
Thoughts pull suffering like engines pull cars.
2 Our minds give life shape; we are as we think.
Good- or ill-thinking: joy or misery.

3 "Angry, they hurt me, beat me, took my stuff!"
Thinking these things, you will be trapped by hate.
4 "In anger, they beat me, hurt me, and won!"
If these thoughts have no power, you are free.

5 See? Hate cannot end hate. Only love can.
6 Remember: this law cannot be broken.
We live life forgetting that death is near.
Remember this law, the fighting will cease.

7 A hurricane will toss a rootless tree.
Death's temptations will toss a rootless dude.
Fear of Death blows away pleasure-seekers.
8 Hurricane winds can't toss a mountain, though.
Death cannot move you if your roots grow deep!
Grow your roots deep in discipline and faith.

9   Polluted thoughts, lies, and lack of self-control
    Cannot be hidden by a saffron robe.
10 Pure thoughts, true words, and self-discipline
    Are worthy of wearing saffron robes.

11 The lost are blinded by meaningless things,
    Which they run after, never finding truth.
12 The smart ones follow that which can never change,
    They follow with clear sight and find the truth.

13 Rain floods through cracks in a broken roof;
    Emotion floods an undisciplined mind.
14 Rain rolls off a well-built and maintained roof;
    Emotion rolls off a disciplined mind.

15 The self-centered suffer now and later.
16 Helping others brings joy now and later.

17 The self-centered suffer now and later.
    They feel the damage now, and more's to come.
18 Helping others brings joy now and later.
    The good that's done is clear, and more's to come.

19 If you do not practice the things you preach,
    You are counting chickens that have not hatched.
    Spiritual happiness will elude you.
20 If you can't preach a word, but know the truth,
    Live beyond craving's control, beyond hate,
    Free of mental pollution, with pure thoughts,
    Then you will live in spiritual joy.

Stanza Two

Watch Out!

21 Be watchful, and Death will have no power.
  If your attention waivers, Death will catch you!
  Work steadily, and Death's power will wane;
  Shirk discipline though, and life will retreat.
22 The real cool dig this wisdom and feel joy.
23 Their calm meditations blow them away
  To the place called *Nirvana*, the blown place.
  Freed from their bonds, they feel great happiness.

24 If you meditate hard, with a clear mind,
  And do compassionate things for people,
  If your inner training is in line with the truth,
  Your acclaim and self-esteem will be real.
25 If you truly work hard at meditation,
  You will be like dry land beyond the flood.

26 The unready folks let their minds wander,
  The smart ones prize having sharp vigilance.
27 Don't let your laziness be permanent;
  Don't make lust your only consistent habit.
  Great joy attends sincere meditation.

28 Sincere work will drive away laziness.
Clever folks march up wisdom's mountains high
Above suffering, as if looking down.

29 Sincere, surrounded by lazy people.
Woke, when everyone else is sleeping.
The smart stand out like winning thoroughbreds.

30 This work is done by even the greatest
Queens and Kings of Demigods and Titans.
Those who try sincerely gain real esteem.
Those trapped in laziness gain no esteem.

31 The hardworking student of the spirit,
The one who stays ahead of laziness,

32 Is like The Human Torch, burning off bonds,
And blowing like smoke toward the big blow-out.

Stanza Three

Thinking

33 As a master bow hunter fires her arrows,
The disciplined control their wayward thoughts.

34 The student's mind, learning meditation
Shivers and twitches like a fish on dry land;
The fibers of our being fear Death's snares,
Our frightened minds run in all directions.

35 The mind loves to wander; it's hard to teach.
To the well-trained mind come joy and wellness
36 Wise minds can make good choices for thought. Yes,
To the well-trained mind come joy and wellness.

37 People who can tell their thoughts where to go
In a way that really sticks the damn things
To where they are told, these folks escape Death.

38 Wisdom cannot live in a troubled mind,
Lacking knowledge of the supporting truths.
39 The smart ones look beyond duality
Their minds are calm and thinking even,
Their eyes are open and they don't feel fear.

40   Do not forget that your body can break.
Your mind can be an unbreakable fort,
Build its walls well and fight Death with wisdom.

41   Bodies return to ashes, dust, and dirt.

42   You can hurt yourself more than others can
With an untrained mind, without discipline.

43   Parents and a whole loving family
Can't help you more than a disciplined mind.

Stanza Four

Blooms

44 A florist picks blooms well and carefully
You should choose to learn the supporting truths
Like the careful florist choosing blossoms.
They will take you far away from Death's grasp,
Further even than the bright fields of the Gods.

45 A florist picks blooms well and carefully
You should choose to learn the supporting truths
Like the careful florist choosing blossoms.
They will take you far away from Death's grasp,
Further even than the bright fields of the Gods!

46 Keep in mind that your body's like beer foam,
Fleeting, like wisps, sundogs, and dust devils.
Keep yourself beyond Death's fragrant bullets.
Then Death and all its ills cannot grab you.

47 A dam breaks, and morning finds a town gone.
They didn't know what hit them, nor will you
If Death finds you gathering the daisies.

48 If you've spent your life on the trivial
Death will knock your feet out from under you,

Spilling all of your distracting flowers.
49 Slip into the depths of meditation
And then out from among its bright petals;
Like the peaceful bee the unharmed flower.

50 Don't count other people's wins and losses
Count your own heads and tails in life's tosses.

51 Those who admonish others and then fail to
Act in the ways they are advocating
Are like silk flowers with no real perfume.
52 Do the good things you tell others to do,
Then you are like a real flower that smells good.

53 One field of flowers makes many bouquets;
One life can do good in many fine ways.
54 Incense and flowers' scent just drift downwind;
The good that you do can be felt all around.

55 All the most beautiful blooms in the world
Cannot rival the perfume of goodness.

56 The white jasmine and the scent of incense
Are weaker than the good in people
To the noses of the ones in Heaven.
57 Those ones, enlightened and sincere and good,
Those ones are always far away from Death.

58 & 59 Real students of The Awoke shine brightly
They stand out beside their sad, burdened peers.
They stand out, just as a lotus stands out
Growing in the most unexpected place.

Stanza Five

Childish People

60 The night drags on and on when you want to sleep.
The road drags on and on when you are tired.
Rebirth goes on and on without support.

61 Take helpful people with you on the path;
Lacking helpful people, go by yourself!
You can't make common cause with sour grapes.

62 The undeveloped stay focused on wealth.
"My family is rich and powerful!"
They are constantly saying to themselves.
When family, wealth, and peace escape them.

63 The childish who know it are just foolish,
The childish who think they are smart, much worse;

64 They don't see the support, no matter what
Amount of time they spend with wise people.
Wax cucumbers will never be pickles.

65 Smart people, hanging out with the right folks,
Will understand the support easily
Like real cucumbers fast become pickles.

66 The childish are their own worst enemies,
Shooting themselves in the foot constantly.

67   If you or other regret what you did,
     If it hurts people for long or short time
     What you did was probably a bad thing.

68   If people are happy with what you did,
     Joyful, it was probably a good thing.

69   The childish think self-centered things are good
     Until they must face the consequences,
     And when they see what happens, it hurts them.

70   Fasting for years, using a blade of grass
     To spoon their food, they are still not yet worth
     A small part of one who has understood.

71   Good cream doesn't go bad in an instant;
     Time sure does tell when an action is bad.
     As hot coals in cold ashes can still burn
     The childish are burned by their actions.

72   If the childish get an idea or two
     They are prone to use them in the wrong way.
     Hurt themselves, and not help themselves at all.

73   Childish people chase false accolades:
     Religious rank, control of the temples, praise.

74   To ascetics and others they proclaim,
     "Listen! Only I know what is right and wrong!
     I am able to do things! You are not!"

75   Go the clearly marked way to wisdom,
     Not the way to false pleasure and profit.
     Students of The Awoke! Do the right thing.

Stanza Six

Enlightened People

76 Someone who helps you avoid a bad way
   Is better than a pirate's treasure map!
   Follow them and find the excellent truths.

77 Listen to that person and take it in,
   Let them help you stay away from bad ways
   Fools will hate them and the wise will love them.

78 Value and cherish honest and true friends.
   Just stay away from dishonest people.

79 To go the way the enlightened ones say
   Brings happiness and peace every day.

80 Farmers shape water by digging ditches.
   Framers shape and nail wood to make houses.
   Fletchers shape wood and feathers for arrows.
   The enlightened farm, frame, and fletch their minds.

81 Accolades and incriminations both
   Blow futilely against the enlightened
   Like hot or cold winds against a boulder.

82 Enlightened minds are transparent and still
   As they hear about the truth of this world.

83   Putting one foot in front of the other,
Enlightened people always keep going.
They don't waste time complaining or gloating
Whatever the winds of fortune bring them.

84   An ascetic choosing celibacy,
Poverty, Humility, not power,
And never worldly success by cheating
Is one to trust as enlightened and moral.

85   Not many people get to the far coast;
They waste their time panicking on this one.

86   If you stick to the truth and true teachings
You will get there, though it be difficult.
You will be aloof from the grasp of Death.

87 & 88   The 'enlightened' are just that: seeking light.
They walk away from the dark and seek light
Willing to leave their familiar haunts,
Willing to eschew gratifications,
Releasing that which they cannot control

89   They achieve emotional purity.
Remembering enlightenment's lessons,
Perceptions under control, freed from greed
They have become truly free. This is light.

Stanza Seven

The Deserving

90 Their journey is done. Sadness is behind.
Life's bonds have no power. Now they are free.

91 The thoughts of the wise are always searching,
Rising like water birds rise from the sea,
And are ever moving on, ever on.

92 How can you pin down a generous soul?
What trail do flying birds leave in the air?
The liberated are as hard to track.

93 How can you pin down these generous souls?
Sensory input does not confuse them.
They eat like birds, too: liberated souls!

94 The divinities are solipsistic,
And they are jealous of those righteous humans
Who have discipline that does not waiver
And hearts unclouded by self-obsession.

95 As solid as planets, as true as gates,
As clear and fresh as a wild woodland spring,
They are now free from reincarnation.

96 Enlightenment brings with it a deep calm,
    Bestowing it on mind, speech, action,
97 Granting inner peace. Self-deception ends.
    Petty attachments end. The truth begins.
    The enlightened have made it to that shore.

98 The enlightened bless the place where they live,
    Urban, rural, tilled earth, or wild ocean.
99 Thoughts free from sensory disturbances,
    Mindful happiness blesses the forest.

Stanza Eight

A Gazillion

100   A gazillion useless and futile words
Mean less than one good word that gives you calm.

101   A gazillion lines of unhelpful verse
Are surpassed by one line that brings you peace.

102   One memorable maxim that grants peace
Outshines all dusty, forgotten volumes.

103   Win the battle to control your own mind,
And you've won a more important battle
Than one with a gazillion enemies.

104 & 105   Win the battle to control your own mind,
A battle not to be fought with others,
And even God cannot take that away.

106   Make one bow to an enlightened person
And you've done more good for the world than if
You'd burned a gazillion pounds of incense.

107   One bow to a wise person is better
Than a gazillion bows to a statue.

108 A year of tithes is not as good for you
As the month's help you give to a wise one.
109 Healthier, happier, prettier and
You'll live longer, too, taking good advice
From and supporting an enlightened one.

110 One day of enlightenment is worth more
Than a gazillion years of confusion.

111 One single day on the path to wisdom
Is better than a gazillion years lost.
112 One day of industry has more meaning
Than a gazillion lazy, idle years.
113 One day of sweet liberty is better
Than a gazillion years of oppression.

114 One peek beyond the grasp of death is worth more
Than a gazillion years of blindness.
115 Twenty-four hours of truth is worth more
Than a gazillion years not knowing it.

Stanza Nine

Sin

116 Do the right thing. Stay away from sinning.
Evil makes you frown, good keeps you grinning.

117 Everyone makes mistakes. Don't repeat them.
It is hard to break out of a deep rut;
Repeated sin makes it hard to break out.

118 When you find an action that is really good
Be happy about doing it again.
Over and over, a happy pattern.

119 A sinner is very happy at first,
Until the wages of that sin are paid
Then they get the sad rewards, and they're fucked.

120 It's the opposite for a good person;
They may be sad just after a good deed,
Then the results of it make them happy.

121 Even the smallest sin has great power;
The first minute of an hour spent outside
Helps freeze you just as much as the last one.

122 Even the smallest good has great power;
The first minute of an hour fireside
Helps warm you just as much as the last one.

123   Help yourself out: stay away from sinning,
       Just as wealthy people stay on the safe roads,
       Just as you would never choose to drink bleach.

124   Infection comes in through an open wound
       And it will not come in through healthy skin.
       Truly free of sin, sin cannot harm you.

125   Hurting innocent people with sin will
       Bite you in the ass eventually.

126   A sinner can be reincarnated
       To experience suffering and pain.
       Reincarnated, those who did good deeds
       Can be given next lives of happiness.
       The truly pure? Blown out like a candle.

127   You cannot fly away, swim away, hike
       Away from the consequences of sin.

128   You cannot fly away, swim away, hike
       Away from the truth that you, too, will die.

Stanza Ten

Payback

129 No one is without terror of payback.
     All humans live in the terror of Death,
     So do not kill any fellow human.
130 They care about living just like you do
     And, yes, payback *is* a motherfucker,
     So don't kill anyone or let them die.

131 Taking joy in hurting other people
     Will hurt you instead, both now and later.
132 If, seeking joy, you do not hurt others
     Also seeking joy, you will be happy.

133 Use gentle words to all those you speak to.
     It will help them think of being nice, too.
     Hurting words will come back to hurt you, too.
134 Tranquil thoughts, like a cracked bell, can't be rung.
     Just be disinterested in conflict.

135 Like a careful cowboy on a long trail,
     Death on his horse Old Age rides beside you,
     Guiding you down the long trail to new life.
136 Selfish deeds are lit matches in the brush:
     Soon the fire is all around, burning you.

137 Don't hurt the blameless or you will suffer
    Sadness, ill health, mishaps, weakness, and
138 Neurosis, civil charges, trolling, and
139 Loss of loved ones, or money problems, and
140 Your house could perish in flames or, worse,
    You could die and burn in the flames of Hell.

141 No amount of prostrating your body
    Can help if your mind is undisciplined.
142 With a peaceful and unthreatening mind,
    Not hurting anyone, sainted, noble—
    Even if they are wearing fancy clothes!

143 Just like you don't need to beat a good steed,
    Good, disciplined thoughts don't need reminders.
144 An enthusiastic embrace of truth,
    Faith, and silent spiritual sitting
    Carry you like a steed beyond sadness.

145 The farmer waters their crops, the hunter
    Aims and fires, the builder cuts and nails boards;
    Just so, the enlightened work with their minds.

Stanza Eleven

The Ruins

146   See the ruins around you while you laugh.
Your laughing body is always dying.
Though it may be dark out, gesture through the flames.

147 & 148   Your physical life is like a drawing
That will fade with time, drawn with Death's pencil,
Blown by your thoughts like papers in the wind.

149   How can we find happiness when we know
Our bones will be tossed out like old pumpkins
After Halloween, buried like compost?

150   And our bones make a frame around our guts.
Muscle, sinew, and skin complete the house;
Vanity, Lies, Decay, and Death move in.

151   The glitziest royal sedan will rust,
Physical vitality passes, too.
The luster of true goodness never wanes.

152   People who spend their lives avoiding thought
Succeed, and die no wiser than a beast.

153 Merry-go-round of reincarnation!
     I have ridden around you many times,
     Hunting for the maker of my body.
     Going around and around is a drag.
154 Now that I have stepped off and seen how it works,
     I won't get back on for another ride;
     The merry-go-round, in parts on the ground,
     With its lights shattered and mirrors broken.
     Selfishness is gone, and I am blown out.

155 Learn to meditate while you are a teen,
     And you'll be prepared to fish in life's streams.
156 Don't get old being unable to fish.

Stanza Twelve

The Mirror

157 Self-care comes from the right kind of love.
It is peaceful to pray for a while at night.

158 Find out the truth then help others find it.
This is the habit of enlightened folks.

159 The first thing to do is to teach yourself—
That's harder, but it prepares you to teach.

160 Self-control is the way to true freedom!
If *you* are your boss, you can trust your boss.

161 Their bad deeds will crush self-centered people
Like diamond crushes the coal, its parent.

162 Evil always hurts the one who does it
Like the killing vine chokes the tree it's on.
It's a trap that traps the one who sets it.
Worse than the traps set by one's enemies.

163 The sins that will hurt you are easy to do,
It can be so much harder to do good!

164   Like the mythical tree that, once it fruits,
       Dies, bullies who fuck with enlightened ones
       And people buying and selling fake news
       Will choke on their own bullshit in the end.

165   Decide to cause harm, harm will come to you.
       To save yourself from suffering, don't sin.
       Every choice you make helps or hurts yourself.
       You cannot make someone else's choices.

166   Please don't hurt yourself to help someone else.
       Care for yourself so that you can give care.

Stanza Thirteen

Locus

167 An unjust law is not worth following
The truth always outweighs authority.
Evil believed by many is still wrong.

168 & 169 Come awake! Smell the coffee! Choose to do
Good, stay away from evil. It will help
You now and in every future life.

170 Life is a soap bubble that's popped by Death.
See it for the illusion it is
And you will be hidden from Death itself.

171 Look all around you at the universe!
Isn't it a hotrod that will break down?
The enlightened ones see through the flash.
Deluded ones can't see through to the truth.

172 When the deluded become enlightened
It is like clouds revealing the bright Moon.

173 When their good deeds take them beyond Evil,
It is like clouds revealing the bright moon.

174 We live in the dark. It is hard to see.
A few of us fly, set free from the trap,
Rising through the firmament to Heaven.

175 Like beautiful birds in a summer sky
The enlightened sail far away from care
Once they have beaten Death and all its tricks.

176 A person who will break the Golden Rule,
Lie, and laugh at reincarnation
Is a person who can do more bad things.

177 Selfish people never go to Heaven,
They would give no joy and they will get none.
The enlightened will try to help others,
Their joy in Heaven is already won.

178 One step toward lasting enlightenment
Is superior even to Heaven,
Far surpasses being a god yourself,
A better crown than all of the worlds'.

Stanza Fourteen

Wake Up!

179   There is no questioning the victory.
      Only the Awoke can claim the great prize.
      How can you reach the perfection of it?
      What path will lead you beyond attachments?
180   What are good ways to talk about the first,
      The Awoke liberated from all cares?

181   The enlightened are envied by the gods,
      Simply sitting has given them such peace.

182   A difficult path leads to consciousness,
      And life as a person is difficult;
      Even more difficult to learn the truth.
      Yet most difficult to be blown away.

183   Listen: do good, and help good to be done,
      Stay away from evil words, deeds, and thoughts.
      Work with discipline to make your mind clean—
      These are the essential lessons. Wake up!

184   Calm concentration will be called patience,
      You should grow it like a summer garden
      That yields the best fruit: you'll be blown away.

185 Refrain from stopping the growth of others,
Hurting others will also hurt yourself.
Follower of the Awoke, be awake.
Do not hurt people's bodies or feelings.
Live by the truth, and don't tear people down.
Eat right, sleep well, and contemplate the truth—
That sums up the lessons of The Awoke.

186 All the money in the world can't fill it,
The hole that your desires have dug in you.
Human desires bring with them human pain.

187 The sublime nectar of the gods is not
Potent enough to extinguish desire.
Controlling your passions is a hallmark
Of understanding The Awoke's lessons.
In controlling desire, you will find joy.

188 When you're afraid, it is tempting to flee
To the woods, or a monastic retreat,
Or another sacred place. Remember:
189 "Fear is the mind killer," and goes with you.

190 The Awoke, The Truth, and The Fellowship
Will help you learn in *Quadveritas*:
191   *One* is that pain is inevitable.
   Two is that suffering is optional.
   Three is that pain and suffering can end.
   Four is that there is a path to this end.
192 In English, that path's *The Octovia*.
To follow it is to end suffering;
The Octovia leads to happiness.

193   It's not every day you meet an Awoke,
      Not just anywhere has one living there.
      Sometimes enlightened ones are born that way,
      Which is very good for the neighborhood!

194   Holy the nativity of The Awoke.
      Holy are the lessons of The Awoke.

195   Holy is the community of faith.
      Holy the peaceful life of the people.

196   Infinitely sacred to pay respect
      To the ones who greatly deserve respect:
      To The Awoke, to their good followers,
      To the ones who no longer taste of fear,
      To the ones free of the touch of Evil,
      To the ones who have left sorrow behind.

Stanza Fifteen

⎯⎯◈⎯⎯

Bliss

197   Let the haters hate; live in happiness.
Live without inner chains, free from hatred.

198   Live in happiness, free from compulsions.
Live clean, even among the addicted.

199   Live happy. Build your strength against illness.
Lie free of chains, though all around are bound.
Live free of greed, though all around are not.

200   Be happy. Don't hold so much you don't need.
Let happiness shine from your face divine.

201   Winning is over-rated; you must cause
The looser sorrow. Better not to play,
And have a calm and happy tomorrow.

202   Sexual desire burns hotter than flame,
Hatred will deplete you more than disease,
Alienation is the worst sorrow,
And great calm brings the deepest happiness.

203   Selfishness is the worst infection; Let
Happiness blow you away completely.

204   A clean body is the finest blessing,
Satisfaction is the finest treasure,
Confidence is the finest family,
Blown away in the finest happiness.

205   Taste the sweet truth as you sit quietly,
Evil and terror will evaporate.

206   Encountering the enlightened is good,
To live with them or near them is the best.
But stay away from the unenlightened
And you'll find happiness more easily.

207   Living your life with the unenlightened
Is like trying to travel with a thief.
Being around the enlightened is fun,
Like being on a fun family trip.

208   And so hang around enlightened people,
Compassionate people, the disciplined,
Easy, happy, calm, and elevated.
Hang with them like the Moon hangs with the stars.

Stanza Sixteen

Obsession

209 Don't forget as you rush to the tasty
Better to meditate than be hasty.
Trapped chasing pleasure and salivating,
You'll wish you spent more time meditating.

210 It hurts to miss seeing something that's good.
It hurts to see something coming that's bad.
So spend some time seeing past good and bad.

211 Let your care for things be free and easy.
Do not grip so tightly that it hurts you.

212 Caring for things the wrong way will hurt you.
It can make you suffer and be afraid.
Find the way to care without fear or pain.

213 A generous love will not bring you pain.
A generous love will never scare you.
Love generously, free from fear and pain.

214 Solipsistic joy always ends badly;
It always ends in some kind of terror.
Stay generous! It will keep you free.

215 Craving bad things will give you the jitters.
Being self-centered is the root of fear.
Being generous brings calm and soothes nerves.

216 Obsession hurts. Obsession brings terror.
Learn discipline to handle obsessions,
And you will be "happy, joyous, and free."

217 Respect rains down on the truthful and good.
Those who have worked to have good character,
Those who work with discipline to know the truth
They bathe in the respect of the whole world.

218 Don't ever settle for easy answers
And your searching heart will never stumble.
In time, you will come to the other shore.

219 & 220 Those who love you are happy to see you
When you arrive at home from a long trip.
The good things you have done will be happy
To see you when you leave this life.
They'll greet you with joy, like those who love you.

Stanza Seventeen

Anger Management

221   You can learn to let go of your anger.
You can free yourself from all foolish pride.
These are handcuffs that you have the key to.
A burning kind of sorrow cannot come
If you don't try to own other people.

222   Control your anger like driving a car
Or it will drive you, asleep at the wheel.

223   Drown rage in kindness, meet lies with the truth,
Selfish acquisition with kind giving.

224   Tell the truth. Do not give anger control.
Give with joy, even if you don't have much.
And you will be given divine blessings.

225   The wise do no harm and have discipline.
They have found a peaceful way of being.
And live very far from sadness.

226   People who keep a sharp, disciplined watch
Over themselves. Training with discipline
All the time, aiming to be blown away
Will gain serenity, past selfish cares.

227   You'll get blamed if you say more than you should.
You'll get blamed if you say less than you should.
You'll get blamed if you say just what you should!
Everyone must get blamed, that's understood.

228   Never in the past, present, or future
Has anyone been all right or all wrong
229 & 230   But even if they are mistaken,
It is hard to call enlightened people "bad,"
It is hard to call wise people "evil,"
Also those who steadfastly meditate.
These shiny pennies are praised by the gods!
Even the utmost god praises those ones.

231   Yes! You can train your body to help you.
232   Gently train your body to follow truth.
Speak to help healing and not to cause harm.
233   Train your mouth to speak gently with kindness
Let Love be the schoolteacher of your mind.
234   Disciplined thoughts, trained body, and kind words:
These are the hallmarks of the enlightened.

Stanza Eighteen

Addiction

235   Winter will come; you will fall like a leaf . . .
And you haven't packed your bags for the trip.
236   It's time to feed the flame inside you,
Time to get right with the fact that it's hard.
You can be clean and sincere. Be that light.

237   Imagine that, moments ago, you have died.
You must travel now without any break,
And yet you have taken no time to pack.
238   Take time to feed the flame inside of you.
Prepare yourself: seek out enlightenment.
Be clean and sincere; you will escape death.

239   Steel is made more pure with each hammer blow,
A bit with each tap, over and over.
240   Rust never sleeps. The harm of evil acts
Will not stop eating you from inside.

241   The verses don't work if you don't say them.
The gods don't hear prayers if you don't pray them.
Houses fall down if you don't maintain them.
Work out your bodies, it will sustain them.
Sleeping watchmen? Dishonor will stain them.

242 To flaunt your beauty dims your beauty, too.
Complaining about a gift spoils the gift.

243 Selfishness spoils both present and future.
Clean your mind! Ignorance is the worst dirt!
Use discipline! Meditate and be clean.

244 Living may seem easy for the lazy
Only spending effort to harm others.
245 Working to live clean can seem hard
It can seem boring until you try it.

246 Murdering, lying, stealing, getting drunk,
To want someone else's money or love,
All will drive nails into your own coffin.
247 Drinking to get drunk will always hurt you.
248 You can hurt yourself so please try not to.
Remember: bad acts bring evil with them.
Learn the discipline that beats selfishness.

249 Real charity has its roots in real faith
And true gifts have their roots in true friendship
Do not give yourself jealousy seeing
Gifts and charity given to others.
250 Envy disappears when its roots are cut.
Cut them with meditation and be free.

251 Lust is the hottest fire that will burn you.
Hate is the strongest chain to enslave you.
Addiction is the most clever trap.
But greed is the river that will drown you.

252 The faults of others are glaring and large;
Our own faults are difficult to see.
We hide our own faults, even from ourselves.

253 But while we are staring at others' faults,
Our own are getting bigger out of sight.

254 The dry leaf is blown where the wind takes it.
The rootless are blown by their own desires.
Follow The Awoken and know freedom.

255 The dry leaf is blown where the wind takes it.
The rootless are blown by their own desires.
Change is the very nature of the world.
Follow The Awoke. Know serenity.

Stanza Nineteen

The Supported Life

256   Violence is never the way of Truth.
257   Call peaceful leaders Protectors of Truth.

258   Number of words is not wisdom's measure,
      Calm discipline's good, patience a treasure.

259   Words are not the foundation of The Truth.
      Even the untaught can uphold The Truth.

260   Sadly, age doesn't always bring wisdom.
261   Honesty, goodness, discipline, kindness,
      And purity of mind make an elder.

262   Beauty can't hide jealousy, lies, or greed.
      Speeches can't hide jealousy, lies, or greed.
263   People without can't hide jealousy, lies, or greed.
      In their minds are really beautiful.

264   A bald head alone does not make a monk
      Out of a person who is filled with greed.
      A razor cannot meditate for you
265   True monks have compassion and selflessness.

266 Living on charity alone does not
Guarantee a contemplative outlook.
You have to discover and follow the truth.

267 The truest kind of monk lives without sex,
And is neither touched by good or evil.
The truest monk is without attachment.

268 & 269 Silence cannot take the place of wisdom.
When you have the chance, choose Good over Bad.

270 True nobility does not harm others;
No creature need fear harm from the Noble.

271 To know who you are, not fake who you are,
Must come before knowledge, meditation,
Celibacy, rituals, and incense.

272 Then you can Wake Up and be Blown Away!
The best, everlasting joy is waiting!

Stanza Twenty

The Octovia

Introduction

This Stanza, often translated as "The Path," or "The Eightfold Way" and "The Four Noble Truths" contains the two lists of ideas that every tradition of following The Awoke holds to be central.

My translation of these two venerable concepts relies on the English language's love of Latin roots and proclivity for neologisms: I call these eight paths "The Octovia" (octo- prefix meaning "eight," and "-via" for "path" in Latin) and "The Quadravera" (quadra- prefix meaning four, and "-vera" the plural of "truth" in Latin).

In the Sanskrit and Pali Support Verses, the Octovia and the Quadravera are to be distilled from the verses in an order that is not how most people are now usually introduced to them. Nor do they have anything like the titles usually assigned to them.

In the interests of helping the beginning student and offering a useful refresher for the established practitioner alike, I have added lines clearly labeling the Octovia and the Quadravera. These lines precede each verse and are in italics. Feel free to ignore them.

In the table below, the Quadravera and Octovia are listed in their now conventional order with their familiar titles, alongside the original verse numbers that correspond to them. In the translation that follows, the verses are presented in this modified order, with the original numbering cheerfully retained in the margins for reference.

The Octovia

The Quadravera

The Octovia:

Right Mindfulness is one of the eight paths.
276   Getting your head straight is something you *do*.
The Awoke is pointing the way for you.
Get your mind right: this is Right Mindfulness.

Right View is another of the eight paths.
277   All things wither and die; "this, too, shall pass."
Know this path and your sufferings will end.

Right Livelihood is what this path is called.
279   Every *way* you are is not *who* you are.
Know this and you are beyond suffering.

To start! This path is called Right Intention.
280 Every day is a good day to start.
Start soon, start young if you can, and start strong.
Pure wisdom is elusive if you wait.
Don't waiver and wait: best to meditate.

Right Speech is the short version of this path.
281 What you say, what you do, and what you think:
Find wisdom by discipline in all three.

This is the path that is called Right Action.
282 Meditation builds a nest for wisdom;
Not meditating leaves no room for it.
Discern for yourself what is not helping
And find out what is making it harder.
Choose your own unburdened way to wisdom.

This allegory is for Right Effort.
283 Set your axe-blade to every selfishness.
One cut down does not complete the whole task.
Fell them. Reveal the path to your freedom.

And this path is called Right Concentration.
286 "Where shall I spend the season? And the next?"
Thinking such thoughts, you will soon lose your way.

The Quadravera:

This is the First Truth that leads to wisdom.
278 Everyone suffers. Know this and be free.

Truth Two: The suffering has these causes.
284 Lust attaches you to life more strongly
Than the calf is attached to its mother cow.

285 Pluck ev'ry selfishness as you would pluck
The dead blossoms from your flower garden.
Step onto the path to get Blown Away,
Go with a teacher to show you the way.

275 *This is the Third Truth:* Suffering can end.
The Awoke said this from beyond sorrow.

The Fourth Truth: this is how suffering ends.
273 Choose The Octovia, eight paths in one.
And the Quadravera: the four best truths.
An attitude of detachment is best.
Human beings who are Awoke are best.
And these four lines are the Four Noble Truths.
274 This path is the true one to conquer Death.

287 Death will take you staring at your paycheck,
Bragging about your car, drinking your drink,
Like a flood obliterating a town.

288 Your family cannot stop your dying.
289 Keep that in mind and get on the right path.

Stanza Twenty-One

A Sampler

290 Owning a measure of serenity
And seeing a way to a larger one,
Leave the smaller to go to the larger.

291 Don't let giving pain to others be the price
Of your joy. It will trap you in hatred.

292 Do not avoid what you know you must do,
And avoid what you know you must not do.
This process will lighten your suffering.

293 Meditation helps you do what you must
And helps you avoid what you must not do.
It helps you to mediate your senses.
It helps you succeed and end your suffering.

294 Kill your lust, though it's as dear as your mom.
Kill your selfishness, as dear as your dad.
Kill your flesh's demands, though they rule you.

295 The Noble have killed lust, though it be dear.
The Noble have killed passions, though it rules,
And The Noble have set ego aside.
A Noble one has been left free from sin.

296 The followers of this guy, Gautama*
     Are focused, awake, and pay attention
     To Him, The Awoke One, round the clock.

297 Gautama's people are focused and clear,
     And Truth is their study all of the time.

298 Gautama's people are focused and clear,
     They gather the people all of the time.

299 Gautama's people are focused and clear,
     Disciplining their senses all the time.

300 Gautama's people are focused and clear,
     In joyful compassion all of the time.

301 Gautama's people are focused and clear,
     Joyfully meditating all the time.

302 It is so painful to be of the world,
     So painful, too, to be out of the world,
     So painful to live with worldly concerns
     And so painful to be lost among them.
     Meditate, meditate, and meditate!
     And the pain will end. you will not be lost.

303 Good seed will grow wherever it is thrown,
     Good people are honored where they are known.

304 The Himalayas' distant, snow-capped peaks
     Seem to sail above the rest of the world.
     Good people shine too, with a distant glow.
     The bad are unseen, like arrows at night.

*Familiar family name of the Awoke.

305   You sit for yourself, you sleep for yourself,
      Your two feet can only move you around;
      Get rid of your own selfishness yourself.

Stanza Twenty-Two

Straight to Hell

306   Broadcasting fake news and denying truth—
Once you are dead, these will be your legacy.

307   Covering up your lack of discipline
With a monk's robe fools no one but yourself.
The evil done this way will hurt you, too.

308   It is better to swallow red-hot iron
Than to sponge off honest charity.

309   If you're married, you should not fuck around.
If you do, people will think less of you,
You'll loose sleep, and it will bring suffering.

310   Your frightened lover and your frightened self
Fearing discovery and punishment
Cannot feel good. Therefore, do not do it.

311   The type of grass The Awoke picked to weave
His meditation mat can cut you, too,
If you hold it the wrong way by mistake.
And good discipline can also go bad
If you use it indiscriminately.

312   The broken promises and careless acts,
      The thoughtless sex when you swore chastity . . .
      These tricks are not helping your discipline.
313   Such shenanigans do not make a monk.
      Commit to the things you say you'll do!

314   Suffering always follows evil deeds.
      Do good deeds so that no suffering comes.
315   Patrol and guard well your walls and defenses,
      Both your internal and external walls.
      A moment wasted is a moment lost.

316   Yes, there are things you should be ashamed of,
      There are things you should not be ashamed of.
      To confuse them is to go the wrong way.
      And to confuse others is the wrong way.

317   Don't fear things you should not be afraid of.
      Fear the things you should be afraid of.
      To confuse them is to go the wrong way.
      And to confuse others is the wrong way.

318   Do not see wrong when there is nothing wrong.
      And you must see wrong when there is wrong.
      To confuse them is to go the wrong way.
      And to confuse others is the wrong way.

319   When you do see the wrong when there is wrong,
      And when there is no wrong, see no wrong,
      Then you will be going the right way.

Stanza Twenty-Three

The Elephantine Stanza

320   It is good to accept insults with patience;
Elephants were known for absorbing blows
Back when they were ridden into battle.
Be tranquil. People are often quite rude!

321   Only trained elephants went into battle.
Queens and kings only rode trained elephants.
Train well to handle insults patiently;
You will find that people of merit do.

322   Trained mules can do a lot of good, hard work.
The horses from Sind can do even more.
And elephants can do the most hard work.
Your trained mind makes you one of the best.

323   Even the best-trained animal can't get
Blown away for you. You have to do that.
Your well-trained mind will carry you to that.

An early story of The Awoke says
That a crazed elephant was sent out to
Kill him, but instead he tamed that wild beast.
The elephant's name: "Danapalaka."

324 When Danapalaka longs for his mate,
He will not eat, though his hunger is great.
Kept from his love in the elephant grove,
He could not break free, though he fought and strove.

325 Eating overmuch and sleeping too late
Like an indolent pig fed for slaughter,
The lazy will be born many times.

326 My mind used to wander off all the time.
Now it is disciplined like a happy
Elephant with a good, gentle trainer.

327 Learn to guard your mind against evil thought.
Extricate yourself out of bad habits
Like an elephant extricates itself
Carefully and thoroughly from the mud.

328 If you come to have a friend who is wise
Who is good, and is a loving person,
Stay on the path with them until it ends,
And walk with them despite hazards.

329 If you do not have that friend who is wise,
Who is good, and is a loving person,
Stay on the path alone, and that is fine.
Be like a king who has retired and left.
Be like an elephant, free in the woods.

330 Better solitude than the company
Of the immature and undisciplined.
Know serenity, like an elephant
Free to live easily in the forest.
Turn your head and walk away from evil.

331 Friends are good when feelings are mutual.
Good things you've done are like friends when you die.
Be a friend to yourself: defeat sorrow.

332 Motherhood is good. Fatherhood is good.
And following The Truth is very good.
It is the most good to achieve wisdom.

333 Virtue is good. Wisdom and faith are good.
A pure mind and a pure heart are good, too!
All of these things will help bring joy that lasts.

Stanza Twenty-Four

Compulsion

334   Stronger than thirst, compulsion will drive you
Jumping like a monkey in the treetops.
Looking for fruit, you jump from life to life.

335   Our compulsions make sorrows spread like weeds.
336   Beat your compulsions and sorrows will run
Off of you like water off the lotus.

337   And so I tell you: pull up compulsion
Like pulling weeds from a kitchen garden
Or Death will break you like the flood breaks sticks.
338   Suffering will grow again and again
If its root, compulsion, is not pulled.

339   If currents flow from your mind to pleasure,
Those strong currents will carry you away.
340   Those currents will flow in all directions
They spring up like weeds. Pull them up quickly.

341 Everyone has insecurities,
The deep thirst for pleasure, and compulsions.
These draw like the tide toward birth and death.

342 The thirst for pleasure drives people like hares.
Scared and suffering, they run back and forth.

343 Find freedom by mastering this thirst.

344 Observe as an example those who are free
Only to be enslaved again by thirst.
Though they were once free, they are again bound.

345 Wood, rope, and steel cannot bind you as tight
As selfishness about kin and wealth can.

346 They'll sink you like being tied to a rock;
Controlling selfishness will untie you.
Seek discipline, let go your compulsions.
Move swiftly in this. Have no second thoughts.

347 You weave the very web that will entrap you
When you let strong compulsions control you.
Escape from the web. Leave cravings behind.

348 Sacrifice what is in front and behind
And release what is in between them, too.
This way you will get to the other side.

349 If you want to get to the other side,
Don't let compulsion make your bonds stronger

350 Know what lasts. Know what is fleeting. Be clear.
Defeat Death by meditating calmly.

351 Someone liberated from compulsions
Is someone who is not tortured by thorns;
They'll no longer know reincarnation.

352 Wisdom contains freedom from compulsion
And grants knowledge of what words really mean.
The ones who are wise know their last body.

353 I have won the contest against myself,
And I live in purity and knowledge.
I am liberated and know freedom.
I have taught myself. Who is my teacher?

354 The Truth is the best gift, and the sweetest.
It brings the most joy and ends compulsion.

355 Greedy people harm themselves with money,
Though not those who seek to get Blown Away.
The Truth ends compulsion and its sorrows.

356 Greed will harm your mind like salt will harm soil,
So honor people who are not greedy.

357 Lust harms the mind like salt will harm the soil,
So honor people who are free from lust.

358 Hate harms the mind like salt will harm the soil,
So honor those who are free from hate.

359 Compulsion harms the mind, as salt the soil,
So honor those free from compulsion.

Stanza Twenty-Five

The Sainted

360 Your senses can be helpful, too, if trained.
Give training to your eyes, ears, nose, and tongue.
361 Actions will give training to your body,
Words you say will give training to your tongue
And thoughts will impart training to your mind.
All of this training will help end sorrow.

362 A real saint's feet, hands, and tongue serve others.
They meditate deeply, and live in joy.
They live at peace with them selves and others.

363 A real saint has a chant that they repeat,
Lives in a simple way, and teaches Truth
With sweet words and patience, and simple grace.

364 A real saint is a follower of Truth,
Thinks about Truth, is joyful about Truth,
And does not ever abandon the Truth.

365 A real saint is contented with what they have
And does not envy what others have;
Jealously interrupts meditation.

366 The Gods themselves will celebrate the saint,
Who lives pure and happy to serve others.
367 They have freedom from the desire to
Own people and things, so they are not sad.

368 A real saint is a teacher and a friend
Passing on the peace of The Awoke One.

369 Saint! Toss the useless weight out of your boat!
Toss out greed and hate. You will be Awake.

370 Toss aside five blocks and five attachments.
You will be light and reach the other side.

371 Saint, you must mediate and meditate!
Let pleasure go. Do not case yourself pain.

372 Meditation can't be without wisdom.
Wisdom can't be without meditation.
To let wisdom grow with meditation
Is to move toward being Blown Away.

373 A saint stills their mind and opens a door
That leads to the peace and joy that is Truth.
374 They know the truth of the mortal flesh.
They know the immortal secrets of Truth.

375 Hey, saint! Keep learning. Train your senses.
Find your contentment following the Truth.
Keep company with the wise and noble
And, as always, know and follow the Truth.
376 Be ev'ryone's friend and do your duty;
You'll know joy upon joy and end sorrow.

377   The cherry blossoms fall when their time has come.
378   Saint. Let your greed and hate wither and fall.
      A saint's thoughts, words, and deeds are tranquil and
      A saint turns away from worldly pleasure.

379   Hey, saint, use your critical thinking skills.
380   Keep constant vigilance over your thoughts
      And joy will come to you; you're your own boss.
      Train your mind as if it was a workhorse.

381   A saint follows truth to the other side,
      Gaining peace and joy beyond daily cares.
382   A young saint who follows Truth is a light,
      Brighter than the moon on a cloudless night.

Stanza Twenty-Six

The Noble

383 Be brave as you cross over the river.
Win the struggle against your obsessions.
See past the bits and pieces of this world
And into life's foundation, beyond death.

384 Be brave as you cross over the river.
Win the struggle against your passions.
Move past love and hate and your chains will fall.

385 How can you tell if someone is noble?
A noble person is past love and hate
And liberated from the bonds of fear.

386 How can you tell if someone is noble?
A noble person will have trained their mind
To tranquility and reached the best goal.

387 The sun's nature is to shine in the day.
The moon's nature is to shine in the night.
The soldier's nature is to shine in war.
The noble's nature shines in meditation.
The Awoke's nature shines with love for all.

388 The noble one has left Evil behind.
And the hermit finds serene solitude.
The pure of heart are a kind of traveler.

389 Call them Noble who do not feel anger.
Call them Noble who do not harm others,
Even when they themselves are hurt badly.

390 Call them Noble who do not hoard pleasures.
Call them Noble who do not cause sorrow.
Even when sorrow has been brought on them.

391 Call them Noble who do not weaponize
Thoughts, words, or deeds and are calm in all ways.

392 Call them Noble who follow The Awoke.
Catch fire from their example burning bright.

393 Not extreme practices and not high birth
Have in them the poser to ennoble.
The Truth ennobles, and love for all life.

394 Why meditate upon a bed of nails?
What do you prove by extreme practices?
What good if your mind is still trapped by lust?

395 Nobility is deeper than a robe,
Deeper than any outward show or sign.
Thoughts and feelings trained by meditation
Grant tranquility and nobility.

396 Class and wealth do not grant nobility.
Freedom from selfishness grants nobility.

397 Chain broken, they are no longer afraid.
Selfishness can no longer threaten them.
Their mind is not cluttered with foolish thoughts.

398 The noble one has cut the bonds of Fate,
Arisen from slumber, and are Awake.

399 Call them Noble who do not fear prison,
Who do not fear death. Love gives them power.

400 Call them Noble who do not feel anger
And do not stop following The Awoke.
They have achieved pure practice and control.
They have received their last incarnation.

401 Call them Noble who do not hold pleasure
As a lotus leaf does not hold water,
Like a pin does not hold a mustard seed.

402 Sorrow will not come to this holy one,
And they shall no longer carry burdens.

403 Call them Noble who are deep in wisdom,
Profound in understanding, and who have
Followed the right path to the supreme goal.

404 Call them Noble who live by humble means,
Who do not practice extreme disciplines,
Nor live daily lives immersed in commerce.

405 Call them Noble who have laid down their arms,
And live in peace with all living things.
They do not kill. They do not help to kill.

406 Call them Noble who are never hostile
Even to those who are hostile to them,
Who are impartial among the selfish,
Who are peaceful among those fighting wars.

407 Call them Noble who have let passion fall,
Self-centeredness and arrogance fall, too—
All fallen away like a mustard seed
Falling down from the tip of a needle.

408 Call them Noble who always tell the truth,
409 Are always kind, asking what they can give
To life, not demanding life give to them.

410 Call them Noble who have entered Heaven,
Freed from selfishness and impurity.
411 No wants, no doubts, complete control of mind
And body, transcending past time and death.

412 Call them Noble those beyond good and evil,
Pure ones, free of sorrow and obsession.

413 Call them Noble, beyond duality,
No sin, no sorrow: shining brightly like the moon.

414 Call them Noble who have crossed the river,
That difficult and dangerous river,
And sit serenely on the other side.

415 Call them Noble who abandon themselves,
Homeless, always at home and contented.

416 Selfishness is gone from the noble mind,
Sorrow has left and it will not come back.

417 Call them Noble who no longer feel greed
Who do not crave even heavenly things,
And who do not have selfish attachments.

418 Call them Noble, no longer tied down
Not attached to people, places, or things.
They are the hero of their own story.

419 Call them Noble for whom "I," "me," and "mine,"
Have lost meaning, who know life's ups and downs.
They are Awake and they will stay Awake.

420 Call them Noble, who are taking a path
Beyond past and future, unknowable,
Where they will never know death and decay.

421 They work for good without thought of profit
Just thinking of freedom for everyone.
Never thinking of pleasure for themselves.

422 Call them Noble who are calm and fearless,
Brave and stable, a Great One of wisdom
Who has achieved the goal of these lives.

423 They have gone across the river of life;
They have completed it and are complete.
It can be said they are one with all life;
All life is in them now, and they in it.

The Buddha, here translated as "The Awoke," was a title conferred on a prince named Siddhārtha Gautama, considered in Buddhist tradition to be the first human to utilize meditation in order to self-reveal the truth of the universe. The Awoke then became a monk in order to spread the realization of the co-arising of wisdom and meditation. Those who first emulated The Awoke's example are believed to have collected the earliest of his sayings in the *Dhammapada*.

Christopher Carter Sanderson is the author of the prose-poetry novel *The Too-Brief Chronicle of Judah Lowe* (Sagging Meniscus), a scholarly book on outdoor theater *Gorilla Theatre* (Routledge), and a translation/adaptation of *Ubu Roi, UBU IS KING!* (Accolades Arts Press). His original poetry appears in recent issues of Griffel, Gravitas Poetry, Poetry City, Poets Choice, and others, and is anthologized in *Show Us Your Papers* (Main Street Rag). His translation/adaptation into English blank verse of *The Beatitudes* of the Bible was also first published in Lunch Ticket Magazine. He is the founding artistic director of NYC's Gorilla Repertory Theater. Christopher has a BFA from New York University, an MFA from Yale University, and is a Fulbright alumnus. He currently teaches writing at the Downtown Writers Center in Syracuse and is a member of the Dramatists Guild. He is also a member of St. Matthew's Episcopal Church in Liverpool, NY and attends Zen Center of Syracuse Hoen-ji.

BLANK PAGE BOOKS

are dedicated to the memory of Royce M. Becker,
who designed Sagging Meniscus books from 2015–2020.

They are:

IVÁN ARGÜELLES
THE BLANK PAGE

JESI BENDER
KINDERKRANKENHAUS

MARVIN COHEN
BOOBOO ROI
THE HARD LIFE OF A STONE, AND OTHER THOUGHTS

GRAHAM GUEST
HENRY'S CHAPEL

JOSHUA KORNREICH
CAVANAUGH
SHAKES BEAR IN THE DARK

STEPHEN MOLES
YOUR DARK MEANING, MOUSE

M.J. NICHOLLS
CONDEMNED TO CYMRU

PAOLO PERGOLA
RESET

BARDSLEY ROSENBRIDGE
SORRY, I BROKE YOUR PROMISE

CHRISTOPHER CARTER SANDERSON
THE SUPPORT VERSES

.

www.ingramcontent.com/pod-product-compliance
Lightning Source LLC
Chambersburg PA
CBHW020216090426
42734CB00008B/1090